# The Unknow methods of Critical Thinking

### Dale Owen

This extends to creating a secondary or tertiary copy of the work or a recorded copy and is only allowed with the express written consent from the Publisher. All additional right reserved.

The information in the following pages is broadly considered a truthful and accurate account of facts and as such, any inattention, use, or misuse of the information in question by the reader will render any resulting actions solely under their purview. There are no scenarios in which the publisher or the original author of this work can be in any fashion deemed liable for any hardship or damages that may befall them after undertaking information described herein.

Additionally, the information in the following pages is intended only for informational purposes and should thus be thought of as universal. As befitting its nature, it is presented without assurance regarding its prolonged validity or interim quality. Trademarks that are mentioned are done without written consent and can in no way be considered an endorsement from the trademark holder.

# Contents

# Introduction

The following chapters will discuss everything that you need to know about critical thinking, and how it can be used to benefit your life in so many ways. Critical Thinking is used to help give us a good idea of how and what decisions we should make, especially when our emotions get the better of us. It can also help you to become a better person and form better relationships with those around you.

In this guide we will take some time to discuss the various elements of critical thinking. We will talk about the ways in which you can benefit from critical thinking, how to go through the different stages and steps to becoming a critical thinker, and how to ask the right questions to help you solve various problems.

We will also spend a little time talking about problem-solving and decision-making. Both of these are very important aspects when it comes to critical thinking and understanding how they work, how they can be of benefit, and how they can improve the way you think.

There are plenty of books on the market about this subject, so thanks for choosing this one! Every effort was made to ensure it is full of as much useful information as possible, and easy to follow. Please enjoy!

# Chapter 1
# Understanding Critical Thinking

There are many things that we often need to think about and make decisions about on a daily basis. Some of these things consist of: what to eat, when to get out of bed, whether we want to try something new, what to get at the store, how fast to drive, whom to hang out with, and so much more. Some of these decisions don't sound of much importance but they can often be the things that can change the course of our whole day or even our whole lives.

Learning how to be a critical thinker can make a big difference in your life. It allows you to look at all of the possible solutions with the information and facts that you have researched. Once you've mastered using your brain's ability to think, you will find that it is easier to make harder decisions a lot quicker. Let's take a look at some of the basics that you need to know to understand how critical thinking works and what it can mean.

## What Is Critical Thinking?

Critical thinking is basically the ability for you to apply reasoning and logic to new or unfamiliar ideas, opinions, and situations. When we learn how to think critically, it means that we can see things in a more open-minded way, and that we will take the time to look at all concepts and ideas from as many angles as possible. While we may not even realize it, critical thinking is an important skill that helps you to take a look past your own views of the world so you can get a better understanding of why people think in certain ways. You may find that you will use it often when you are in a debate so you can form better arguments for your side.

The ability of thinking in a critical way is essential. It helps you to create new possibilities when it comes to problem-solving. While there are a lot of people who are against critical thinking, it is actually a method that allows you to be more open-minded because you have to seek out different answers to a current problem you are working with. You also need to be willing to accept an answer, even if it isn't the one that you were planning on hearing.

Open-minded thinking requires that someone is not going to assume that their own approach is the right way or the best way. They have to be willing to take different steps or a different course of action no matter what it is. For example, if you were a scientist, you would need to be open to the idea that when you do an experiment, you will always have to be open to a result that you probably were not expecting

Being open minded will allow it to be much easier for you to find out new things and discover more than before. You won't be limited by the limiting beliefs you had going into it to start with. This can be a challenge in some cases, but you will find that it provides you with tremendous and meaningful discoveries that you would have missed out on in the past.

Another part of critical thinking that you need to pay attention to is the ability of the person to approach any situation or problem rationally. Being rational requires that you analyze all of the information that you know. From there, you can make analyses and judgments based on evidence, rather than on your own emotions and opinions.

An honest approach to reasoning means that the critical thinker needs to acknowledge their own emotions, motives, and personal goals and realize that these are going to have some influence on your opinions and on the way that you think about things. Rational thought can sometimes involve finding and then getting rid of any prejudices that you already have. This helps you to be objective and can bring a fresh approach to any problem that you may encounter.

In many cases, critical thinking is going to rely on your ability to take a look at the world in a way that won't focus on your personal self. This can be something that doesn't come easy to most. We are already in our own minds, having emotions, thoughts, and experiences that can color the way that we see things. But we end up letting these things color our own experiences and the way we feel about things determine the decisions that we make day to day.

Being able to empathize with a person means that the thinker must be able to stop thinking about themselves for a short amount of time, and instead put themselves in the place of someone else. This can help you to learn cooperation, teamwork, and communication skills when you use more empathy. This is why empathy, as well as critical thinking skills, are so valuable in many professional fields.

So, how do we use this? An effective critical thinker, to begin with, is a thinker who takes the time to analyze what they know about the subject. They will need to make the extra effort to recognize what they don't know about a topic. This can form an initial knowledge base for consideration. The thinker can take some time to look at what research is out there about the subject. It is their job to identify what they can learn, just by looking over all of the research that is out there.

Often the skills that you need to develop to be a critical thinker are the same as what you can find in science. A scientist can take a close look at what they see in the world, makes a prediction (while still keeping themselves open-minded enough to accept answers that may be different from that prediction), and then they go through and try to find all the information to either prove or disprove your theory in the end.

When you try to take this approach in your own personal life, you will learn how to place more emphasis on finding the preconceived notions and prejudices that you already hold. This allows you to work in eliminating and even avoiding these opinions so that you can come up with a more objective or honest review of any issues. This can be applied in many different scenarios that you encounter.

Having the ability to think in this manner can help you out in so many ways. You can actually think things through properly. You will take a look at all the facts and make an informed decision. You refuse to allow your prejudices, and your emotions take over and make the decisions for you. This helps you to make the best decisions for your needs and can make it easier for you to form lasting and healthy relationships in your personal and professional life.

Critical thinking can be used in many different ways. Students may use it to evaluate the plot of a book or when they want to figure out the motives of a character in a literature class. Someone on the debate team would have to spend time thinking about a subject in a critical manner to form up a strong argument and anticipate all of the points that their competitors would try to make. Many people are going to use empathy and open-mindedness in their personal lives to help them get tasks done as effectively as possible and to make it easier to work as a team.

Critical thinking can be used in many different areas of your life. Learning how to use it on any situation that you encounter can make a big difference in how you approach a situation, how you get along with others, and so much more.

# What Are the Critical Thinking Skills?

There are a lot of different skills that you need to have when you want to work on your critical thinking skills. Let's take a look at the top seven critical thinking skills that you can work on:

1. **Analyzing:** This is when you will need to take the information that you receive, break it up or separate it into parts so that you can discover what the true nature, functions, and relationships are all about.

2. **Applying the standards:** This is when you are going to take the information that you received and then choose to judge on it according to rules and criteria that are already established.

3. **Discriminating:** This is when you can take the time to recognize the similarities and differences among situations and other things. Then, you can take each one and give them a category or a rank based on what they fit in the most with.

4. **Information seeking:** This is when the individual will take his or her time to search for evidence, facts, or knowledge. This can be done by looking for relevant sources and gathering the best data from the sources that you have.

5. **Logical reasoning:** This is when you will need to draw some conclusions or references that are supported with the help of the evidence that you found.

6. **Predicting:** This is when you envision a plan and some of the consequences that may come

with it before making your final decision about it.

7. **Transforming the knowledge:** This is when you will convert or change the condition, nature, form, or function of concepts for different contexts.

## What Critical Thinking Involves

To start, critical thinking is going to involve a lot of logic, but when we look at the definition, we are looking more at truth compared to logic. Critical thinking involves a sort of reflection on what we are being presented in terms of information. We get to look at that information and decide whether we should accept that as a valuable idea, an action, or behavior, rather than letting others tell us what to think. We can look at the situation objectively, regardless of our current moods or who presented the information to us in the first place.

For example, you may decide to watch television late at night. During this time, you may see a lot of commercials for various food joints around town. When we stop to ask ourselves whether it is a good idea to go out and pick up some junk food early in the morning or not show that we are using this kind of thinking. We may take some time to draw up reasons why we should and shouldn't do it, leading us to weigh out both sides and make a decision.

It is important to remember that just because we are using critical thinking doesn't mean that we will always make the right decisions. Sometimes, we try to use this critical thinking and then we come up with the wrong or maybe just a bad conclusion. We will need to do the math to help us figure out if we are reaching the right answer.

Now, there is also a thing known as non-critical thinking. This is a bit different than you may think when you look at the other options. To start, non-critical thinking is just the absence of being engaged in the process of critical thinking, but it doesn't necessarily mean that you are being dumb or irrational.

We may spend more time working with non-critical thinking on a regular basis because it is easier to do. If you never think critically, then this is going to cause some issues, and you may miss out on a lot of opportunities. But, sometimes, such as when you are listening to music or playing a little game with someone else, the non-critical thinking or thinking that doesn't mean you to use analysis to can come up with the solutions that you need.

## Qualities and Characteristics of Critical Thinkers

Critical thinkers view the world in a different way than most of us are used to. They will take a look at a situation or any decision that they are faced with, and take the time to consider all of the different options before they make that final decision. They will solve a problem in a manner that provides the best results, not the solution that has always been used.

But what are some of the most common characteristics found in someone who is considered a critical thinker? There are a number of traits that you will find in these individuals, and some of the characteristics may surprise you a little. Let's take a look into some of these traits, and the things that you can even work on to help you to improve your thinking game.

The first trait is curiosity. Those who are critical thinkers are very curious about a lot of different topics, and they often will have a very broad interest. If you find that only few things interest you, and you don't like to look up or research into things, then you may need to work on your critical thinking skills. Critical thinkers tend to have a healthy amount of inquisitiveness about the world and even about other people. They may even have an appreciation for and an understanding of the diversity of beliefs, cultures, and views found in the world, even if they vary from their own. This is one of the reasons that they are great lifelong learners.

They are also known to have compassion. While critical thinkers are often mistaken as people who have no feelings and who don't empathize well with others, this couldn't be farther from the truth. Many times, these thinkers act just as much with their hearts as they do with their minds. They understand that the world is already full of a ton of segregation and judgment; you can't do much without having someone nearby who is ready to judge on how you do it. More than often, these negative things are going to happen due to a lack of understanding of how each person approaches a problem.

For example, someone from a different part of the world may have a different worldview than you. Someone from the city may have a different viewpoint compared to someone from the country. Someone with two parents at home will see things differently than someone who has just one parent at home. Each of us have our own story that makes us who we are. We all also have our own challenges and trials that have worked to shape and make us a unique individual. People who can think critically can recognize these different histories, and they will compassionately celebrate all of the uniqueness found in everyone. They can also see the best in themselves and in others.

Next, we need to take a look at the characteristic of awareness. Opportunities to apply your skills in critical thinking present themselves all the time. Effective critical thinkers will remain tuned into this fact, and they will keep themselves on high alert for any chance that is needed to apply the very best thinking habits no matter what situation they are in.

You will find that the best critical thinkers do not take anything they hear or see at face value. These are the people who will keep on asking questions, and they will continue to explore each and every side of an issue to find the right decision. This makes many of them instinctual problem solvers simply because they are aware that they need to always research and figure out the right answer for themselves.

Decisiveness can be a great trait for many critical thinkers as well. A lot of decisions need to be made quickly throughout your life. When you are a critical thinker, you can take the time to weigh out all of the options and then imagine the outcomes right then and there, with lots of clarity and speed, without wasting time. There are many instances where regular thinkers will take too long to make a decision, this will often cause them to miss out on something.

There are even some situations where we must make our own decisions, even if the information we need isn't there. When you face any kind of challenges, there is a chance that someone will need to take the lead, leading them having to make some hard decisions, ones that many others will shy away from. Many times, the critical thinker realizes that, sometimes, it is necessary for them to take the initiative and make the hard decisions, even if they end up being wrong. To a critical thinker, it is much preferable to not making a decision at all.

Critical thinkers are also honest. Moral integrity, global citizenship practices, and ethical consideration and action are all traits that you can find in a critical thinker. Honesty is found in each of these things. We see in such people a strong desire for fulfillment and harmony in the world, and part of being able to attain this will involve pursuing honesty in all relationships and endeavors that we try out.

As a critical thinker, you must always strive to use honesty in the things that you do. It isn't going to help you come up with truth and integrity and a good conclusion if you try to build it upon lies and falsehoods. When you are working on your critical thinking skills, you need to make sure that you are not only dealing with honesty when you talk to others but that you search out the truth and honesty at all times in the information that you are given.

There are a number of key considerations that can include flexibility and willingness for a critical thinker. These can be included in, but certainly are not limited, to things like the ability to:

1. Learn from your own shortcomings and mistakes.
2. Challenge the status-quo if they see that there is a need.
3. Be open-minded and learn how to embrace others' opinions and views, even if these end up challenging their own views and opinions.
4. At times, reconsider and even make some revisions to your own opinion if you are shown new evidence that may contradict what you are basing your conclusions on.
5. Listen in an active manner. Critical thinkers do not enter into a conversation just waiting for their own turn to talk, without actually listening to what others say.
6. Always learn, always improve, and always excel.

And, of course, you will find that critical thinkers are very creative in their thinking as well. Creativity is very important when it comes to the modern workforce and when it comes to our personal lives as well. Critical thinking in professional, marketing, and business alliances often relies on your ability to be creative. When businesses get a chance to be creative with their own products and even add in different ways of creativity in the way these products are advertised, they are more likely to do well.

## Examples of Critical Thinking

When it comes to critical thinking, a lot of examples and ways can be used to help improve your life. You can use it at work to come up with new solutions to problems that are troubling everyone. You can use it as a way to think through all of the different scenarios that you encounter in your life so you make decisions that are the most informed. There are very few instances where critical thinking wouldn't serve you well. Some examples of when you would be able to benefit from critical thinking include:

1.  If you encounter a friend who is angry, you can use critical thinking to help you interpret what that person needs. Even though that person is mad, they are still showing their needs through their comments and emotions. A critical thinker can step in and determine what the person actually needs, rather than just getting upset by it all.

2.  A manager may encounter a dispute between a few employees and decide that they need to be as objective as they can. They will listen to both sides and weigh them out using critical thinking to provide a fair option for all sides.

3.  A team of scientists who are working on a complex experiment needs to have great precision. This helps them to gather and analyze data to help them out.

4.  A creative writer may need to use these skills to organize all of the ideas they have for a plot of

a story. They need to keep a lot of things in line when it comes to the motivations that show up and the various personalities of fictional characters.

5. A person who is running a small business has to use a lot of research and their own critical thinking to determine any possible human and economic consequences of various ways to reduce costs and increase sales.

6. A student who needs to be able to correctly explain the methodology that they used in order to come up with their conclusion.

7. An educator using various questions to ensure that their students are going to get new insights from the lesson.

8. Judges, juries, lawyers, crime scene analysts, and police detectives taking the time to investigate, interrogate, and do the rest of the things that are needed in order to serve justice.

9. An applicant who takes the time to prepare themselves for an interview may have to use

critical thinking to explain their skills and experiences and why they should be hired for the job.

10. Any parent who is trying to anticipate the costs of having a family or sending their child to college. They may do an analysis of their projected income and then budget to put money aside for this cost.

11. A financial planner can use their critical thinking skills to anticipate the impact of new income tax legislation on the tax liabilities of their client.

## Thinking Hiccups

There are a lot of different things that can cause issues when it is time to think in a critical manner. Perhaps we don't understand the whole situation completely and we have decided to let that block our judgment. Maybe we come into the situation with a negative outlook from the start, and we refuse to let our biases sit to the side. Maybe there was some kind of traumatic event that came into play that changed our perceptions and made it hard for us to think in a critical fashion.

Most experts agree that there are four main roadblocks that can stop us from thinking things through in a more critical manner. Sometimes, these will create some negative feelings about getting more involved in the process of critical thinking.

The first major roadblock is that we feel critical thinking is more of a negative process. We may feel that this type of thinking is going to just tear down ideas, without inserting something in place of those original ideas. In actuality, this critical thinking is a very positive process. It helps us to take a look at the ideas that we are presented with in a more realistic way. We can then determine, without as many biases, whether we would like to believe those ideas or not.

Another issue is that we think critical thinking will make it impossible to make any commitments to ideas or people in our lives. We think that we will spend so much time thinking critically that there is no way that we could commit to others and have meaningful relationships. In reality, you can still make commitments to others; these commitments just become more informed than before so we're not only helping others, but we also agree with ones that fit our own needs and benefit us as well.

You may find that some people will see critical thinking is more of a traumatic change. The reason for this is that we think we need to always abandon old assumptions to think this way. But in reality, you can keep all of the old beliefs that you want when you start thinking in a critical manner. You will learn how to make decisions that are more informed, rather than just being consumed by your original beliefs. You don't have to give up anything; you can now just back them up with proof because you have thought things out.

And finally, another issue that many people have with critical thinking is that they think this involves being cold, unemotional, and detached. There are many critical thinkers out there who are compassionate and emotional towards others. You can easily do the same. Critical thinking can actually help you be more compassionate and helpful to others, and many find that it is liberating compared to their old way of thinking. This is often due to the fact that critical thinking allows us to free ourselves from our past assumptions and frees us from the anxiety we feel with self-scrutiny.

## How Can Critical Thinking Benefit You?

Critical thinking is much more than a concept. It is a real-life model that you can use in order to build up efficient and successful problem-solving skills in your own life. You will be amazed at how much these new skills can benefit you in the workplace, in your personal life, and more. While critical thinking can be a system that is misjudged as a type of criticism, this is far from the truth. In fact, critical thinking allows you to be more open as you'll more than often want to take your time gathering all the facts before you make any decisions.

There are a lot of benefits that you can enjoy when it comes to critical thinking. The first one is that this is a crucial learning development that allows you to be more aware of the different approaches you can take to solve one problem. Without critical thinking, you are most likely to go with the method of problem-solving that is the easiest or the one that is seen as most standard. But with this skill, you will be able to find other approaches, sometimes ones of more value.

The critical thinking mindset allows you to save time. With this mindset, you will already know that all the information out there isn't going to be that important or relevant to your decision-making process. While some people are not sure how to filter out the relevant content and information from the irrelevant stuff. Critical thinking makes it easier to prioritize your time and resources by analyzing the information and finding what is most essential to the process. This can help to speed up the process while also allowing you to make a decision that is the best for your needs.

As a critical thinker, you will be able to gain an appreciation for all different types of viewpoints. This is because, even if you don't believe the same thing as others, you can learn how to empathize with the point of view that they have. Critical thinking enables you to see beyond your cultural norms, without judging them, so you can learn the different factors that may influence your own decision-making process, as well as others.

Another benefit of critical thinking is better communication. By using this skill to analyze and build up evidence for any given premise, critical thinking ensures that you become a more effective communicator than before. Having consistent and relevant points to ensure you can support the theory you are following can be very important in communicating with other people.

Of course, when you work with this, you also increase your own decision-making abilities. You will keep the guesswork and the intuition out of the mix. These may be right in some cases, but without facts to back them up, they are just guesses and are not a part of the critical thinking process. Instead, you begin to work on a more analytical and considered basis, which ensures that you have sounder decisions.

Something that you can gain from this also is that you will learn more reasoning. There are two types of reasoning: deductive and inductive. Critical thinking will teach you how to pick the right one for the situation. Grounding decisions in logic and reason, rather than on your instincts and your emotions, which can vary, will ensure that you are effective at problem-solving no matter the situation.

As you can see, there are a lot of different benefits that come with critical thinking. Every person who decides to challenge themselves to become a better and more effective thinker, and can dedicate themselves to these new skills will be able to experience all of these benefits for themselves as well.

## Can I Really Use Critical Thinking?

Yes, everyone can use critical thinking in their lives. This kind of thinking ensures that you can handle any situation that comes your way, and make it easier for you to handle any situation in a fair and objective manner. You will be amazed at how well this kind of thinking can benefit your life if you just learn how to develop this skill.

There will be times when critical thinking is beneficial to you, and other times you may find that it actually slows you down. Understanding which one fits into each category can be a great sign of a critical thinker. For example, when it comes to picking out the outfit that you want to wear for the day, you don't really need to employ the skills you are learning with critical thinking. Just pick out the outfit you like the best or the one that makes the most sense for what you are doing that day.

There are many situations that can utilize your thinking skills. Being able to employ some of the skills we discuss in this guidebook and to utilize critical thinking properly can help to take a ton of weight of your shoulders. For example, if you encounter a big problem in production at work, you may need to employ critical thinking in your life. If you are trying to decide which college you want to go to, where you want to live, or what career you want to pursue when you have a few options, then critical thinking can be useful.

An effective critical thinker knows when they need to employ this kind of thinking and when it is best used to make a decision without the need to over think. This ensures that you will actually make the right decisions in your life, without having to worry about wasting a ton of time in the process.

# The Main Components of Critical Thinking

Every process is usually made up of essential components, and critical thinking is exactly the same. These components provide you a structure to the process, which, if incorporated the right way, makes persuasive, truthful, and supportive verbal communication possible to the high influence, others' points of view, and message acceptance.

There are several different components that come with critical thinking including: perception, assumptions, emotion, language, argument, fallacy, logic, and problem-solving. Let's take a look at each of these components and what they can mean when it comes time to your thinking process.

❖ **Perception:** The first component that comes with critical thinking is perception. This is the way in which individuals can receive, interpret, and then translate the experiences they have. How each individual perceives things around them will define how they are able to think through a situation. The past history that you have, your current mood, and the way a situation is framed can often influence your perception. Perception is interesting because it often provides individuals with a filtering system.

❖ **Emotion:** No matter how hard you work to think in a critical manner, your emotions will come into play at least a little bit. Your emotions are a part of everything that you do and everything that you think. Emotions are the biggest cause of creating and putting into place the operating and thinking barriers. These barriers can often be used as a way to defend us against the world. Whether that is healthy or not maybe dependent on the situation, but the emotions still have some say in how this goes. Critical thinkers don't have to ignore these emotions, and they don't even need to deny that the emotions are there. They just need to learn how to manage and accept these emotions.

❖ **Language:** Your thinking can't be separated out from the language. Both of these have three main purposes that go together and these include to explain, to inform, and to persuade. Language denotes (or designates meanings) and connotes (or implies or suggests something to the other person), and it relies on a lot of metaphors in order to get the job done.

Metaphors can be very powerful tools in language, and in some cases, when they are used properly, they can even influence the way that an individual thinks and solves a problem. These tools in speech can sometimes give a lot more depth and color to your language compared to other things. Metaphors can be many different things including poetic renditions, stories, and short phrases. Understanding how others use these tools and these different types of languages can help you to take a step back from them and determine whether there is actually something of value being said or not, and whether you should follow what they say or not.

❖ **Argument:** For our purposes here, an argument is a claim used to persuade the other person that something is either true or untrue. It can sometimes be used to persuade someone to do something. For something to be considered an argument, there need to be three basic elements. There needs to be an issue present or one or more reasons for you to consider. There also needs to be a conclusion.

Now, just because someone presents an argument doesn't mean that it is valid. All arguments can be either be valid or invalid based on the structure that is with them, and only the premises and conclusion are reached, which can neither be false or true.

The goal you are working towards when you use critical thinking is to implement sound arguments into your life. This ensures that you have both a valid or a proper structure in your arguments and that these arguments are going to contain true premises. This is where critical thinking and all the logic make a big difference.

❖ **Fallacy:** If you are using reasoning that doesn't meet the criteria that has been set out for a sound argument, then that reasoning is going to be seen as erroneous or fallacious. This kind of fallacy comes when the individual uses the wrong patterns of reasoning. This doesn't always mean that they have a false conclusion, but it can underscore the fact that all of the reasoning that the individual used to support that conclusion is not valid.

❖ **Logic:** Logic incorporates two methods of reasoning, namely inductive and deductive. When we take a look at deductive reasoning, we are looking at the kind that relies on validity, certainty, facts, a truth in the premises, sound arguments, and conclusions that are supported.

On the other hand, inductive reasoning is a bit different because it will rely on probability, diverse facts, generalizations, and even hypotheses depending on the situation.

Often, we will use logic to help us solve the problem. Just like any other kind of problem we encounter. Using logic to solve a problem requires:

1. Understanding the problem. It means we need to listen, read, and take heed to know what is going on.
2. Identifying all of the known and the unknown, rather than trying to hide from all the unknown.
3. Interpreting any relationships that come between the known and the unknown. Sometimes, you may find that working with a visual aid can make the problem-solving easier.
4. Repeating the process any time we find it is necessary.
5. Generating a strategy to help us think logically.

6. Applying the strategy that we come up with.

Critical thinking is such an important part of our lives. If we don't take the time to increase our thinking and to become more critical about the facts that we are presented, then a lot of our beliefs may be wrong, and we may make decisions based on facts that are untrue. We will take some time later on to explore this a bit more, but understanding some of the basics of critical thinking, as we talked about in this chapter, can help us get started.

# Chapter 2
# Critical Thinking Test

Everyone can benefit from working on their critical thinking skills. You will find such benefits like it being easier to get along with others, able to learn the best ways to look at different solutions that are present for a problem and know how to pick the right one. You will also become more open to the different points of view you encounter from different people around you

Before you can determine where you want to go with your critical thinking skills and if there are any improvements as you work on developing your skills, you need to have a good benchmark of where you are starting. This chapter will take a look at some of the ways that you can test your own critical thinking skills and help you find ways to improve it overall.

# The Critical Thinking Test

Now that we have more of an understanding about what critical thinking is all about, it is time to do some testing to see how good your own critical thinking skills are. While there are a lot of different variations on the definition that comes with critical thinking, the one that works best for our needs is this type of thinking that has the ability to comprehend the logical connections that occur between concepts, phrases, words, and ideas.

Everyone has a different level of critical thinking, and you can always work to try to improve your own thinking skills so you can develop these traits and characteristics as well. But most of us have no idea where our thinking skills are at when we first start. How are we supposed to increase our critical thinking when we have no idea where we are getting started from?

We are going to start out with some simple questions you can answer which will give you a good idea of how good your critical thinking skills can be. You can use this information to help you get a good bookmark of where you are in the beginning, then you can work from there.

Critical thinking requires the individual to learn how to recognize a pattern in the information they are given. It is especially important for that individual to recognize how the information can be connected back to the real world. Here, we are going to take a few examples to help you see how these tests work. Go ahead and try them out for yourself!

The first part will include the five words below:

1. Automobile (not a race car)
2. Walking on foot
3. Airplane
4. Bicycle
5. Cruise ship

Now, you want to start by putting them in order, from the slowest to the fastest. We will assume that they are going at their fastest speed when we do this. Go ahead and do that now, there could be different solutions to the problem. For example, you will find that the solution here has the cruise ship going faster than the car, but you may have an argument that the car is actually faster. This is known as indeterminacy and can come into play often during critical thinking.

There are also different kinds puzzles that are a little more straightforward, such as the one we have here. Take not of these words in your head:

1. Navy
2. Sky
3. Celeste
4. Azure
5. Cerulean

What do you see with these words and what do they have in common? All of the words refer to different shades of blue.

Now, take a few minutes to go through the next seven puzzles that we have here. These will hopefully be a little bit more challenging for you. We will include the answers at the end, to help you check how you are doing when it is all done.

You will want to have a pen and paper ready to note down your answers as we go along.

What do the five things listed below have in common with each other?

1. Beer
2. Orange juice
3. Soda pop
4. Coffee
5. Milk

If you took the following buildings and listed them based on their height, going from the smallest to the tallest, what would their order be?

1. Shed
2. Skyscraper
3. Duplex

4. Bungalow

5. Camping tent (a typical one, not a deluxe or special one)

What do the animals listed below have in common?

1. Mouse

2. Squirrel

3. Raccoon

4. Fox

5. Cat

Take the inventions that we have listed below and make sure to list them out in order, going from the earliest to the most recent.

1. Radio

2. Television

3. Gramophone

4. Telephone

5. Telegraph

What feature can you find with the words below that they all have in common?

1. Understand
2. Over
3. Imagination
4. Egg
5. Armchair

Looking at the bodies of water that we have below, put them in order based on their volume, starting with the smallest.

1. Lake
2. Pond
3. Ocean
4. Brook
5. Sea

When you look at the following land masses, what do you see them having in common with each other?

1. Sinai

2. Istria

3. Karpass

4. Gallipoli

5. Italy

Now that you have had some time to take a look at the questions and write down your answers, let's take a look at the answer sheet to see how much you were able to get right.

1. These are all drinkable liquids.
2. 5, 1, 4, 3, 2
3. They are all quadrupeds, and they have a tail. Also, they are all mammals.
4. 5, 4, 3, 1, 2
5. All of them start with a vowel.
6. 4, 2, 1, 5, 3
7. All of these land masses are peninsulas.

This is just a simple test that you can work with to give you a general idea of your thinking ability. But try not to worry if you struggled with this, it's not the end of the world, there are many ways you can improve your thinking skills which we will go through later in this book. If you wanted to test your ability further there are also different tests online or even with professionals that can help you look at various aspects of your critical thinking, such as your personality and how your emotions can factor into the mix as well. But this is still a great place to start to give you an idea of how your critical thinking skills are doing.

## How Often Should You Test Yourself

The answer to this one varies based on how much time you spend on the techniques and how much improvement you think you are making. No matter who you are though, it is always a good idea to get started with a test right from the beginning. This can be difficult for some people because they will feel nervous about taking tests and seeing how bad their critical thinking actually is. But no one else has to see the result. This is just a number that you can use to compare yourself to other thinkers, and it may be a great way you can use to stay motived any time when things get tough.

From here, you are going to have some freedom to the number of times you want to test yourself. Testing often, in the beginning, is a good idea. Maybe consider doing a test every other week for the first few months. This can provide you with a chance to see how quickly your skills are improving and can provide you with some motivation to keep on going with the work.

Over time, as you start getting into the groove with critical thinking and you have been able to see how well your skills have improved, you can choose to limit how many times you want to further test yourself. You should do it often enough to keep yourself motivated and working, but it doesn't need to be done all the time. Many times, testing once a month or once every six weeks can be more than enough to keep you on track, and help you to see how effective your work is.

During this process, keep a notebook or something you can use to write down the critical thinking scores as you go. There will be times when you are working with this kind of process where it feels like you aren't making any progress. It is hard to remember what your score results were down the line when you want to compare things. After each test, especially for the first test that you take, make sure that you write down the answers of what you get. Even if they only provide you with a result rather than the answers, it can still help you to get the information you need to improve.

## Different Types of Thinking Tests

There are many critical thinking tests that can work when it comes to testing your ability. You will want to make sure that you find an effective one that is suited for your needs. Doing research is crucial when finding the right test, so will need to be sure that you find a test that is hard enough to make your brain actually engage, and one that has a reputable research team or company behind it to make sure that this test is legitimate. Also it'll need to be long enough in order to actually provide you with some real results in the end.

You also want to take a look at whether the company provides a few different types of tests that you can choose from. Try to test yourself on a regular basis to see if your critical thinking skills are getting better. If you do the exact same test each time, you will simply start to memorize the answers, and get caught up in thinking in the same sort of thinking cycle which causes a lot of issues with the validity of the test. Or, if you end up using a different test each time, then your results are not going to be consistent between the two.

If you can find a test that has different options but comes from the same company as you used originally, this will make it easier for you to work through your techniques and the process and still test yourself on a regular basis when you want to. When you can do this, you will be more than often amazed at the results that you get, and you'll find one of the best ways to track your results and your improvements.

## Are Some Tests Better Than Others?

Some of these tests are going to be easier to complete and others will be more difficult. The good thing is that you'll get the option of picking out which test you want to use. If one seems too easy for your baseline, then try something more difficult to work with.

As you are searching around for the test that you want to use, make sure that you pay attention to where they are sourced from, what kinds of questions they ask, how long they are, and even any reviews that you see. If the test looks like something for fun from a popular magazine, then you may want to avoid it and go with something else. If it comes from a popular book or from a reputable company or research group, then this is the best option for you to start with.

## How Can I Tell If I'm Improving?

Taking these tests at regular intervals and writing down the results that you get will ensure that you are actually getting better with your critical thinking skills. Find a test that you rely on and stick with it. Skipping between one test to another or at least tests by different companies can mess with your end results. Since they are all different, it is likely that you are going to get varying answers to how you are doing, making it harder to tell if you are actually making progress.

In the beginning, take some time to research the different tests out there. You can even take a few of them to see which one you like the best. Once you have that, take the time to go through and work on one of the tests to get a baseline score. When you are done, write that score down so you have something to compare to later on.

Many people don't write down their score because they are worried about how low it is, or they think that they'll remember the information in their heads. Don't fret about where your critical thinking score is right now. The whole point of this guidebook is to help you improve this skill. It is less important to focus on where you are now than it is to focus on where you want to go. This result is simply so you can get an idea of where you started, and then you can see how much you increase over time.

## How to Identify Critical Thinking Issues

All of us have a belief that we are great at critical thinking. We often believe that there is no chance we will be taken in by things that people tell us. We think that we are smart enough to sort through everything we see and hear and determine whether the information is true or false. We think that we can form a good argument against others, and that there is no way that we need to do more research and take more time to become a good critical thinker.

The truth is, we usually are not as good at critical thinking as we believe we are. Thinking in critical ways means that we need to assess all of our decisions and beliefs with a thorough examination. We need to seek out all the information available to us and ensure that any of the conclusions that we reach are well-reasoned. While there are biases that can and will show up sometimes, a critical thinker will understand these and avoid them, while using implication and logic to make it better and to still choose the right decision in each scenario.

You may be a good critical thinker in some areas of your life, but it is likely that one or more area is going to suffer to some extent. Here, we are going to take a look at some of the areas that critical thinkers can often have trouble with.

The first high issue area for critical thinking is self-assessment. As many studies show, humans aren't the best at judging their own progress. We often rate ourselves lower or higher than we need to most of the time, whether we are considering our skills, the knowledge that we have, or how well we did on a test. Going on your own feelings and what your emotions tell you to do can really make it hard to think in a critical way. No one has ever made the best decisions when they are highly emotional. If you ever find yourself feeling down on yourself, you may self-assess yourself less than you should, compared to if you were in a good mood, you may self-assess yourself at a higher level than you really should.

The truth is, even when you are working with critical thinking, you may find that it is hard to self-assess yourself. This is why people take before and after pictures when they are trying to lose weight, and it is the reason we take tests to look at our skills. Sometimes, we think we have come further than we have, and sometimes we think we haven't made any progress at all. Having these benchmarks and testing yourself is one of the best ways to determine if you are actually seeing progress or not.

Another thing to watch out for is the statistics and probability. Most people are not very good at judging the odds of a decision or understanding how statistics can be applied in the real world. Sure, you may have learned a few statistics and probability in math class, but when you are trying to assess the probability, you may find that the amount you want to see can be a much bigger factor than anything else. Most of the time we are not taught about using an appropriate sample size, how to deal with the outliers, and many other things needed to apply statistics in real life.

Some people run into issues with recognizing any biases they may have. If you take a look at some of the studies out there, you may notice that there is a common idea that people have trouble knowing when they are making errors in their judgment and when they are being biased. While we can quickly recognize these issues in others, sometimes, we run into trouble spotting these in ourselves which can make it to make good decisions ourselves.

When there is a bias in your thinking, it is hard to change your mind no matter how many facts you encounter that goes against it. Critical thinkers have to be willing to give up the notions they have in the beginning if there is enough evidence to prove you wrong. It is fine to have some guesses or notions in the beginning, but holding onto them just because you don't want to believe something else is not a good sign. There is nothing wrong with having a bias, and most people, no matter how hard they try, will start out with some thoughts on a subject. But the difference is that a critical thinker is still willing to take in both sides and will be willing to change their ideas if needed.

You also need to worry about how your emotions can come into play with the thoughts that you have. If your emotions are negative at the time or you are more attached emotionally to one option over another, it is harder to pick another option even if that other one is the correct one. This can be seen a lot with the relationships that we have. We may know that a relationship is toxic and bad for us, but because we are attached emotionally to that other person, we choose to stay. We may know that the other person is right with a decision, but because we don't like them or they did something to us in the past, we refuse to see reason and stick with the outside, even when it is the wrong side.

If you want to be a critical thinker, then you need to recognize how your emotions come into play and learn how to make smart decisions, despite what your emotions are saying. This doesn't mean that you can't ever feel an emotion, but as a critical thinker, you have to make sure that your emotions are not controlling the decisions that you make.

Even some of the best critical thinkers are not going to be immune to some of the issues above. Everyone can face them at some point or another. It is up to you to determine whether they keep you from making smart decisions or not. Understanding what these issues are and learning how to avoid them and work against them will ensure you make the best decisions possible.

# Chapter 3

# The Steps and Stages of Critical Thinking

There are many different parts that come to the process of critical thinking. You may fall into several different stages based on the way you approach a problem and its solution right now. There are also different steps that you can choose to follow when it comes to becoming a critical thinker in your own life. Let's take a look at each of these and how they all work together to come up with the best way for you to become a critical thinker.

## What Are the Different Stages of Critical Thinking?

As you work on becoming a critical thinker, you will find that there are a few different stages of critical thinking that you need to consider. Depending on how far you are in the process, you may fit into one of the stages. In the beginning, you may be an unreflective thinker, but as you work on your skills, you can move into an accomplished thinker or at least an advanced thinker. With that said, there are six main stages of critical thinking, which will be explained below. These include:

1. The unreflective thinker
2. The challenged thinker
3. The beginning thinker
4. The practicing thinker
5. The advanced thinker
6. The accomplished thinker

## The Unreflective Thinker

To start with is the unreflective thinker. These individuals are usually unaware of the determining role that their thinking can have in their lives. They will often run into a lot of problems because the current method of thinking they use leads them there. Unreflective thinkers may lack the ability to assess their thinking, so it is hard for them to improve it.

You will find that an unreflective thinker lacks the knowledge that they need to think critically. They may just make decisions based on their emotions or on a limited number of facts. They won't take the time to look through different points of view, assess their thinking, do research, or anything else to ensure they make the best decisions possible. In some cases, these types of thinkers can develop skills for thinking, without even being aware of it. But since these skills are applied in an inconsistent manner, it doesn't really help them out all that much.

## The Challenged Thinker

A thinker can move over to being challenged when they are first seeing that their thinking is playing a role in their lives and when they are aware of the fact that the big problems that come up in their thinking can cause them significant problems. They are just starting to see the difference and starting to see that high-quality thinking means that they need to be deliberate with their way of thinking. They may see that their current way of thinking is flawed, but they may not be able to identify these flaws.

Most thinkers who fit in this stage are going to be limited when it comes to skills for thinking. They may have a few skills although they aren't aware of them and these skills will sometimes get in the way of their development of becoming more advanced thinkers. Many of these thinkers have found ways to make themselves believe their thinking is much better than it really is, which can sometimes make it more of a challenge when it comes down to trying to improve their thinking skill.

## The Beginning Thinker

When an individual starts to move to this stage, they are ready to take on the challenge of improving their thinking through different domains of their lives. Thinkers who enter this stage know that they have problems with the current way that they think, and they are starting to take the right steps to better understand the ways in which they can improve their thinking. They may even might try to make modifications to their thinking, but their insight is limited right now. They may not have a good plan for improving their thinking, so many of their efforts are lacking and not that helpful.

Beginning thinkers are aware of their thinking and can even understand how their thinking plays a role in their assumptions and points, of view. They are just starting to recognize that there are many standards to asses their thinking and that all of these need to be in place to see results. These thinkers may even be able to appreciate someone critiquing their powers, and their skill level is high enough that they can start to monitor their thoughts, even though their monitoring may not be the best.

## The Practicing Thinker

Thinkers who have moved into this stage usually have a sense of the habits that they would work on to be in control of their own thinking. They recognize that there are problems blocking their thinking and are ready to attack these problems in a systematic way. Based on their sense of the need to practice on a regular basis, they are actively looking at their mode of thinking on several domains. Since they are only doing this in a systematic way, though, they may be limited on their insights.

The practicing thinker has enough skill when it comes to thinking that they can now critique their own plan for systematic practice, and they can then critique their own powers of thought. They can also work to monitor their own thoughts on a regular basis. This helps them to articulate effectively their own weaknesses and strengths. They may even be able to recognize their own egocentric thinking and see the same in others.

## The Advanced Thinker

Thinkers who have been able to move onto this stage are now establishing good habits or thoughts that pay off for them. Based on these new habits they have, they can analyze their thinking on all of the domains of their lives, but they are still lacking on the significant insights into problems at a deeper level of thought. They can think well across many different dimensions of their lives, but they may not be able to consistently do this.

Advanced thinkers are actively and successfully engaging in a systematic monitor of the role of their thinking in all options. They may critique their own way of doing things to ensure they think fairly and critically. They have a great knowledge of the qualities of their thinking, and they can often identify when their thinking is more egocentric than not. They may even have a few different strategies that they can use to limit how much this happens.

## The Accomplished Thinker

An accomplished thinker has not only taken charge over their thinking, but they know that they need to continuously monitor their thinking, revising it, and thinking of new strategies to make it better. They have internalized the basic skills of thought so that all the critical thinking they do is now highly intuitive and easy to work with. They will do a self-assessment on a regular basis, and they know how to be fair-minded and can usually control their own egocentric nature rather than letting it take control over them.

Thinkers who fit into this category often critique their own use of thinking throughout their lives and will normally try to find a way to improve it. They can monitor the thoughts they have and know their strengths and the weaknesses of their own thinking. They still have a bit of egocentrism that sneaks into their thoughts on occasion, but they are usually able to control this, rather than letting it take over and control the way that they think altogether.

# What Are the Different Steps of Critical Thinking?

We also need to look at the different stages and steps that come with critical thinking. Each day, we are faced with a multitude of problems and situations that we need to solve after a thorough evaluation, and with these situations, we are often challenged to understand the different perspectives that we need to think about to get the right solution.

Most of the time we will build up our cognitive thinking based on what has happened to us in the past. However, this doesn't always mean that we will always come up with a better solution to a problem. This may be due to the fact that a decision can be affected by the wrong facts, our emotions, or some other external influences that determine the solution we pick. This is why critical thinking tends to build on a rational, open-minded process that will depend on information and empirical evidence.

The beauty of critical thinking is that it can help us to think through the decisions rather than jumping right to a conclusion. Instead, critical thinking can guide the mind through a variety of logical steps that will ensure that we take in a larger range of perspectives, even if these are different from our own. From here, we can accept the finding, put aside the biases that we personally have, and then consider from all of the possibilities that are possible.

Now, there are six steps that you can use in order to achieve the results we have just mentioned. These include knowledge, comprehension, application, analyze, synthesis, and then to take action. Let's take a look at a brief description of each of these and some of the ways that you can implement each of these to help you become a more critical thinker.

## Knowledge

For every problem that you encounter, a clear vision is one of the best ways to get on the path to solving that problem. In this step, we are going to figure out what argument or what problem needs to be solved. If we don't have a clear picture of the problem that we need to solve, how are we ever going to stand a chance of looking for the right information and figuring out the right way to solve it.

To start, you need to ask the right questions that will help you acquire a deeper understanding of the problem. You may even find that when you are asking questions, there isn't really an actual problem, which means there isn't much of a need to move forward with the other steps in your critical thinking model. Do you really want to spend a lot of time working on a problem and finding a good solution for it if there really isn't a problem there to start with?

When you are thinking about the questions that you want to ask in this question, remember that open-ended ones are the best. These allow you to really explore the problem. Answering yes or no to a question may be easier for you, but it doesn't really provide you with any of the information that you need to solve that problem. When you ask the right questions, you will give yourself a chance to discuss and explore the main reasons behind it. During this stage, there are two big questions that you must address no matter what else you ask later on: What is the problem? Why do we need to solve it?

## Comprehension

Once you have taken the time to ask yourself questions and figure out what the problem is, the next thing to work on is understanding the situation and the facts that are aligned with it. You have to fully comprehend the problem and gather as many facts as you can to help you determine the best course of action. It is impossible for you to figure out a good solution if you don't even comprehend anything about the problem.

The data that you collect about the problem can be found with a lot of research. You can choose the kind of research methods that you want to use. You may also find that the deadline you get can make a difference as well. If you have a month to figure out a solution, then you may be able to explore your options more than if you are only given a few days to do the same.

Make sure that when you are doing your research, you find research that comes from many different perspectives. It isn't going to do you much good if the information that you collect only leans towards your own opinion on the matter. If you are going to do it this way, why not just pick your solution from the start and save time? A critical thinker wants to be able to find the best solution, regardless of what that solution is. So, try to find a lot of different perspectives to help you make all decisions.

## Application

This step is going to continue on with the previous step to help you get a complete understanding of the different facts that are aligned with it and the data that you took the time to collect concerning the problem, using whichever research method that you want. You can then take this research and use it to solve the problem at hand by building up links between the resources and the information.

You may find that a mind map can also be helpful when you want to analyze the situation. A mind map is type of visual diagram using a bunch of ideas that all lead to one central overall idea. You can then use the information on your mind map to come up with the best solution.

## Analyze

Once you have taken the time to gather the information and have linked together everything that you can between the main problems, it is time to analyze the situation. You will want to take some time to look at the strong points, all of the weak points, and the challenges faced when it comes to solving the problem. You can also use this time to set up the right priorities for your main cause so that you can determine the best way to address them in the solution.

This part can take some time. During this time, you will need to find tools that you can use to make the analyses easier to work on. For example, one tool that can be used to help with this step is the cause-effect diagram. This divides the problem away from the causes of the problem aiming to identify all of the different causes so that they can be categorized based on their type and how much they actually impact the problem at hand.

If you are dealing with a big problem, you may need to take more time to analyze. The cause and effect chart may be bigger than you anticipated.

## Synthesis

When we reach this stage, we will have taken the proper time to fully analyze all of the problem and have considered all of the information related to it. We can now work on forming a decision on how to solve the problem. As we come up with a solution, we can look at the initial routes to follow to make this decision so we can put it into action.

You may find that with some of the more complex problems, there could be several solutions. If you see that there are a few solutions to a problem, you need to evaluate them and then prioritize which one seems like the best option to help you pick the right one. Depending on how big a problem this is, you can use a SWOT analysis or something similar to it in order to identify the strength, weakness, opportunity, and threats to each solution.

## Take Action

The final step that we need to look at here is taking action. By now, you should have come up with a solution that you can put into action in order to handle the problem. You can then take the result of your critical thinking and turn it into actionable steps. If you find that the decision involves a certain project or team, then you need to go through and do a plan of action to make sure that the right solution is adopted and executed the way that you would like.

Now, sometimes, you will have a fair bit of time to go through all of these steps. You can take a few days or even a few weeks to consider all of the different options that are available and go from there. Other times, you may just have a matter of minutes to make a decision based on the information that you have been given and your situation. Regardless of the amount of time that you have to make a decision, you can still work with the basics of critical thinking to come up with a good solution. The only thing that'll differ is the time you'll get to do research and analysis. But as you learn to adapt to this thinking process, you will eventually be able to make faster decisions as well.

# Chapter 4
# How to Develop Your Thinking Skills

At this point, you should now have a good idea of what critical thinking is all about. You know that it is important to help you get the results that you want in making the best decisions to improve your life, and that there are also different steps and stages that come with critical thinking.

We are now going to take a look at some of the best practical ways that you can develop your critical thinking skills in your everyday life to get the best results possible.

## Ask Basic Questions

The first thing that you can work on is asking basic questions about any problem or situation that occurs in your life. Sometimes, the explanation of something becomes so convoluted and complex that you lose out on the original question that you should be asking. In order to make sure that you are avoiding this, you continually need to go back to the basic questions that you asked when you first made it your goal to find a solution to the problem.

Every problem that you encounter along the way has a different set of questions that you can ask. You should always ask more and more questions to help you out. The more questions that you can ask about a specific problem, the more viewpoints you can get for it, and the easier it becomes to see the right solution show up. But some of the key questions that you can ask to get yourself started no matter what the problem include:

1. What am I overlooking about this problem?
2. What information do I already know?
3. How do I know this information? Am I able to trust this source?
4. What am I looking to prove or disprove or critique with this problem?

# Question Some of Your Basic Assumptions

Some of the best innovators throughout history were those individuals who were able to look up for a moment and wonder if the assumptions that everyone else were using were actually wrong. When you question the assumptions that you and others make, this is when innovation is going to happen. Of course, you don't have to be an Einstein or anything to benefit from making a question the assumptions that are out there. What about that trip that you have wanted to take? The hobby that you want to try? The internship that you wanted to get?

All of these things can actually become a reality for you, but you do need to step out of your comfort zone, question your assumptions and then critically evaluate your beliefs about what is possible, appropriate, and prudent.

You always want to be careful about the assumptions you are making in your regular life. There are a lot of assumptions out there about a lot of things and just following along with them, without taking the time to review why those assumptions are there and whether they are right or wrong, can lead to a lot of problems. Sometimes, the assumptions are right. But more often than not, they are wrong. Realizing this and looking for a better solution can be one of the best things you can do.

## Being Aware of Your Mental Processes

Human thought is pretty amazing. But the automation and the speed that happens in some cases with this thought process can be a disadvantage to us when we want to think in a critical manner. Sure, it was there to help us survive and do well in the past. But now that we are in a time and age where we aren't always in danger, this kind of mental process doesn't always serve us the best overall.

Our brains are set up to use mental shortcuts, also known as heuristics, to help explain what is going on around us. This happens automatically, even if we don't actively think about it. This was very beneficial to us when we were fighting off animals and hunting large game. But when we need to take the time to think through something critically, it can be a disaster.

As a critical thinker, you need to be aware of this cognitive bias and the personal prejudice that we have. We need to realize that this can make it hard to be objective and come up with the actual best solutions and decisions. All of us are born with this bias when it comes to our thinking, and it's not something that we can fully avoid. But when we become aware of these issues and work to fight against them, it can help drastically towards improving your thinking ability.

## Try Reversing Things

If you are stuck on a hard problem and you just can't seem to find the right solution to solving it, then one thing that you will want to try out is reversing things. For example, you may find that it is obvious that X causes Y, but why not look and see what would happen if Y caused X.

A good example of this issue is the chicken and the egg problem. At first, it may seem like the chicken coming first is the obvious answer. The chicken is responsible for laying the egg so it makes sense to think this way. but then you stop and think that the chicken had to come from somewhere, and since chickens come straight from eggs, it also makes sense that the egg had to be the first to come.

In some cases, this will answer the problem and you will even be able to come up with the best solution a lot easier. Of course, there will be times when the reverse is not true. But taking the time to consider it can help you change your way of thinking, and it may be just the trick that you need to actually find the right solution.

# Evaluate the Evidence That You Have

Any time that you are working to solve a problem, you will find that it can be helpful to look at other information that others have done previously in the same area. It is likely that someone, at some point, has encountered the same problem, and this will be able you to see a lot of the information and research that you need to make a good solution. There really isn't a reason for you to go through and start solving a new problem from scratch, especially when others have already been able to do a lot of the work on that problem for you ahead of time.

You are likely to find a ton of information and research out there that you can use when it comes to evaluating the problem. However, it is also important for you to take a critical look at the information that you find. Not all of the information is going to be informative, not all of it will be complete, and not all of it will actually be truthful. There is often a lot of bias out there when it comes to the information that you want to use, and you must be aware of this.

For example, you may find that there is an article out there that bashes the benefits of one natural remedy or natural medication that you can use for diabetes or blood pressure. It may sound convincing, and if you just looked at the document, you may believe that you need to stay as far away from that natural solution as possible. But then you take a closer look and find that the researchers who did the study were funded by a big diabetes medication company, and now you know that maybe the medication isn't so bad, but maybe it will cut into the profits of the big company.

When you find evidence that you want to use or evaluate, you need to ask questions. Look at who took the time to gather the evidence. Look at the way that they gathered the evidence, and then ask why they gathered this information. This can go a long way in helping you determine whether the information is a good source to work from, or whether you need to find something with less bias in it. Finding out the information to these questions doesn't automatically discredit them, but it lets you know whether there is any form of bias in the information before you choose to use it.

## Always Think for Yourself

While we have spent some time talking about the importance of research when it comes to critical thinking, make sure that you don't become so bogged down in reading and research that you decide to just use someone else's thinking, rather than your own. You always need to think for yourself. In fact, this can quickly become one of your most powerful tools.

Sometimes, the best way to make a decision is to not listen to the opinions of someone else. This can get you bogged down and, in some cases, you may find that the emotional ties of a certain situation can make it really hard to find someone who isn't biased. Thinking on your own and using the information that you already have at your disposal, instead of looking for other opinions, can be the best bet.

In fact, even Einstein thought that this could be the best way to think about situations over others. C. P. Snow, after writing about Einstein for some time, observed that it was like Einstein "had reached the conclusions by pure thought, unaided, without listening to the opinions of others". This was in regard to Einstein's paper "On the Electrodynamics of Moving Bodies". If Einstein chose to come up with his own conclusions without taking a look at the opinions of others, then so can you.

Of course, this doesn't mean that you should be overconfident. There are times when you still need to bring out the research of others and listen to other opinions to help you with your own decisions. But you can also recognize that thinking for yourself is really important when it comes to answering some of the tough questions that you must deal with. Knowing the right times to deal with each one can make a big difference in how well you are able to think critically.

## Not Always Needing to Think Critically

Thinking critically is so important when it comes to making the right decisions for your own life. It can help you to make decisions that will benefit you and can even help in building your professional and personal relationships. However, you won't be able to think critically in every situation you encounter.

It is fine to not think about each and every decision critically. But critical thinking is an important tool that you can use. Just like other skills and tools that you may work on in your life, it is one that you should deploy when you need to solve really difficult problems or when you must make important decisions. But this doesn't mean that you need to take the time and energy to think critically about every decision.

For example, there is no reason to think critically about what you will have for lunch. Unless you have some sort of food allergies, you can just make a decision based on how hungry you are, what is nearby, and what sounds good. Most people decide their lunch in just a few minutes or less, and this is perfectly fine. It's unlikely that the one meal out of thousands in your life will make that big of a difference.

But when it comes to making big decisions, such as changing to a new job, deciding where to live, buying a home, and so on, then critical thinking can be very important. It is your job as a critical thinker to figure out the best times to think critically and the times when it may not be as necessary.

# Chapter 5
# Questions to Apply in Critical Thinking

When it comes to critical thinking, asking lots of questions can help you get the results you need. The more questions that you ask, the easier it will be for you to figure out all of the possible solutions to an issue. When you are picking out questions, you must make sure that you apply questions that are open-ended. It isn't going to do you much good if all of your questions can be answered as yes and no. Doing this will only limit the answers that you get back and the information that you find out.

It is always best to use questions that require you to think, take a little time to discuss, and need more than one-word answers to complete. You can always utilize the five why's that we talked about earlier, or you can find another method that works the better for you, as long as you ask lots of questions and ensure that they need a lot of discussions to go with them.

The type and number of questions that you choose to ask will directly relate to the problem you are dealing with. Some may work well using the five why's helping you to get the answers you need to solve the problem. Other times, you may need to make more time in order to answer more questions to find the solution. Critical thinkers know that the first solution they come up with or the first question that you ask won't give you the best solution possible most of the time. Asking more questions to help you with the certainty of the answers that you get can help you out a lot. Let's take a look at some of the questions that you can ask when it comes to critical thinking.

## Knowledge

The first part that we are going to look at is the knowledge questions. This is going to allow the individual to exhibit information that they have learnt in the past. They simply can do this by recalling basic concepts, terms, recalling facts, and answers. Some of the questions that you can ask that fit into this category include:

1. How would you describe…?
2. Why did…?
3. How would you explain..?
4. When did X happen?
5. What is…?

## Comprehension

It is also possible for you to use your comprehension with these questions. Being able to demonstrate an understanding of facts and ideas can be possible with the help of organization, translation, comparison, interpretation, and giving descriptions. You can also use this as a way to state your ideas. When your able to use all of the other options, you will get better at stating your ideas because you  have the facts to back yourself up. Some of the questions that you can use that fit into this category include:

1. What evidence is there?
2. What ideas or facts do we have?
3. Explain the situation or the answers in your own words.
4. How would you compare or contrast?

# Application

Now, it is time to move onto the application of the solution and some of the questions that you need to ask to make this work. Being able to solve problems by applying any of the knowledge that you acquired can be a part of this. You also have to take a different view of the rules, techniques, and facts that you encounter during this time as well. Some of the questions that you can ask when you are in the application part of the process include:

1. What might happen if I do X?
2. What approach would be the best to do X?

3. How would you show how well you understand X?

4. What examples can you find?

# Analysis

During the analysis, you will take a look at all of the information and research that you looked for to examine and break down information into smaller parts. This helps you to identify motives and causes. You can also spend this time making inferences and find evidence that will support your generalizations. Some of the questions that you can ask when you are looking through this analysis category include:

1. Are you able to identify the different parts of the category?

2. What is the best way to categorize X?

3. Are you able to classify X?

4. Are you able to make any inferences?

# Evaluation

During this category, you will need to present and then defend your opinions by making judgments about the information you have, the validity of ideas that you are looking at, and the quality of work based on the criteria that you set. Some of the questions that you can ask when it comes to the evaluation category include:

1. What would you recommend to someone else if you had been…?
2. What was the value or the importance of…?
3. What is the contribution of X to the whole process?
4. Which option do you feel is the best?
5. How would you compare X to other options?

# Creation and Synthesis

At some point, you will need to be creative with the solution that you have. This part requires that you compile together information in a different way than before. You can do this by taking the elements that you have and combining them into a new pattern. You can even spend some time proposing new and alternative solutions that others may not have considered in the past. Some of the questions that you can consider for this section include:

1. Is there a marmite solution that you can go with here?
2. Are you able to propose an alternative interpretation to that of X? what might have happened if?

Asking a ton of questions during this process is going to help you to come up with new solutions that can work well for your problem. You never want to stop with just one or two questions. This may provide you with one or two solutions, but this doesn't guarantee that you are going to find the best one. Asking questions about different things and looking at the problem in different ways can ensure that you will be able to find the solutions that you want and need for that particular problem.

# Chapter 6
## Decision-Making

Another aspect that we need to talk about when it comes to critical thinking is your decision-making abilities. Critical thinking isn't going to do you much good if you cannot put it to work in making the best decisions for you. This chapter will help shed some light on decision-making and why it is so important aspect that you need to master in your daily life.

## What Is Decision-Making?

For the most part, decision-making helps you to solve any problem that you encounter, whether it happens in your personal life or in your professional life. You will do this by examining all the choices at your disposal and then deciding on the best way to fix that problem. Many people find that using a step-by-step approach is a great way to make thoughtful and informed decisions that will have a positive impact on you.

There are seven basic steps that can be utilized in the decision-making process, no matter what kind of decision you are trying to make. These seven steps include the following:

1. **Identify the decision:** You first need to stop and recognize the problem and make a decision that actually addresses the nature of the problem. Determine why this decision is going to be so important so you can stay on the right track from the beginning.

2. **Gather the necessary information:** The next thing to work on is to gather any and all information needed so that you can make smart decisions based on relevant data and facts. This will usually take some work. You need to look at the information and determine if it has any value, if it is relevant to the decision you want to make, and whether you need more information or not. During this stage, ask yourself what is needed to make the right decisions, and then seek out anyone else who

may need to be involved in the decision-making process.

3. **Identify all of the alternatives:** Once you have taken the time to get a clear understanding of the issue, it is time to look at all the different solutions that are present. No matter what the decision, it's likely that there will be several solutions. You can take a look at the options at this point and use that to determine the best course of action at this time.

4. **Weigh all the evidence**: After you have the different solutions at your disposal, it is time to weigh the evidence and determine which solutions will actually be the best for you. For each solution, you will want to go through and weigh the pros and the cons, and then pick out the option that will provide you with the least amount of risk. You may also want to consider a second opinion during this time.

5. **Choose your solution:** When you reach the time to make a decision, make sure that you

really know the risks with each chosen route. It may even be possible to choose a combination of alternatives if the information and the risks point to this being the best option.

6. **Take action:** The point of doing these steps is for you to be able to take the necessary action needed. Once you pick out a good solution, you will need to come up with a good plan for implementation. This can include identifying what resources are required and then getting the right support that is needed, if this is necessary.

7. **Review the decision:** After the solution has had time to be implemented, it is time to evaluate how effective the decision is. You can then make any improvements that are needed.

At times, decision-making can be hard, and you will find yourself struggling to stick with one over another. You will want to make sure that you are picking out the solution that works best for you. We always want to find a way to use the solution that has the lowest amount of risk and the biggest amount of positives for us. Then, there are times when the emotions come into play or the one with the least amount of risk is harder to accomplish, and we may often struggle against that in the hopes of finding a better solution.

Following the steps that we just talked about to come up with the best solution will ensure that you actually find and stick with a good decision when your deciding on something. Having this systematic method of looking for the best solution will also help you to keep emotions out of the way.

Although the steps that we have just mentioned make it easier to come up with the most effective decisions, there are still a few pitfalls that you may need to watch out for. The first one is that you either have too little or too much information. Gathering the right information is so important when you start with the decision-making process. As a critical thinker, it is your job to figure out how much of this background information you truly need. Too little and it is hard to make a smart decision; too much and you may feel overwhelmed often leading you to confusion which will prevent you from making the decision that you need.

Another issue that you may encounter is that you misidentify the problem. Most of the time, you will be able to correctly see the issues around the decision. However, there may be times when the decision is more complex, and you will have trouble figuring out where this main issue is. Take the time to speak with experts, conduct research, and more to help you figure out the right problem. This, in the long run, is going to save you a ton of resources and time.

Sometimes, the issue that you will face with your decision-making is that you are overly confident in the outcome you will get. Even if you go through all of the steps we have talked about, there is a chance that the outcome won't turn out the way you want. Being overconfident can lead you to making mistakes and make it harder for you to handle if the solution doesn't end up being the one that you've expected.

# Things That Can Affect Your Decision-Making

There are a lot of different things that can come into play with your decision-making abilities. You have to be very careful when you are trying to make important decisions because there are a lot of things that can come into play that will help you to make better decisions, or that can also make it hard for you to work on your decision-making abilities.

The first thing that can affect your decision-making abilities is your emotions. When you let your emotions out to play, you are less likely to make the decisions that are right for you. Instead, you will choose things based on whether you like someone or not, or make decisions in the heat of the moment, often with no thought or logic behind it. Learning how to make decisions without the emotions is so important when you are a critical thinker.

Another issue to watch out for is whether you have the right kind of information, and the right amount, to help with making a decision. If you try to make a decision without any information at all, or if you pick out information that is wrong or biased, you will often have a lot of trouble making the right decision. You should always be careful when it comes to your decision-making process to ensure you actually have the facts that you need.

Your physical comfort can also affect the decision-making process. If you are tired, hungry, uncomfortable, or in pain, then you may need to work on fixing these issues. Your mind is going to head right over to the physical ailments before it tries to make any important decisions. So, take a nap if you are tired. If you are hungry, eat something beforehand and make sure you get a drink. Work to reduce the amount of discomfort you have before you work on any major decision.

If you are tired or fatigued from making a lot of decisions, it can affect your decision-making skills as well. If you have spent all day thinking things through and coming up with decisions about various problems, your mind will tend to glaze over. It may be wise to put off the decision-making for a while and take time out so you can give your mind a break to ensure your mind can go back to being fully optimal when it comes to thinking and making decisions.

# How to Make a Decision

We run into making choices each day. There are times when we choose the wrong things, and there are times when we struggle to make a decision at all in the first place. If you find that this is a problem you are dealing with, then it is time for you to learn some techniques that will help you in making better decisions. Some of the steps that you can take in order to increase your decision-making skills include:

## Determine What You Have at Stake

There are a lot of decisions you need to make in your life. Choices can range from something huge that can change your life all the way to something as simple as trying to pick what to wear in the morning. Being able to determine the weight of all your decisions can make it easier to complete these decisions. This is a pretty basic aspect of thinking you can apply. If the decision is a big choice, then it requires some research and more careful consideration. Smaller decisions, such as what to wear in the morning, can just be done on blind faith and what you prefer because there isn't as much weight placed on those. Ask yourself a question in these situations such as: "Is this really a big decision that I need more time to think about? or am I over thinking this as it's something that doesn't really matter too much?"

## Why Are You Making the Decision?

There are certain agendas and reasonings that can effect the overall decision that you come to make. To help determine who the decision is for and who may benefit from the decision the most, you have to really think through it and consider the decision from many different angles.

This again brings up the idea of asking a lot of questions. First, ask if there are any other reasons why you need to make this decision. Is there anyone in particular who will benefit if you make a certain decision over another one? All of this information can make it easier for you to help you achieve the reason for making a decision and may even make it easier when it comes to choosing the right one also.

## Determine the Number of Choices You Have

With a lot of the decisions that you need to make, there is going to be at least two choices that you can choose from. And more than often, these choices can even be hidden. For example, even if you are doing something as simple as picking out a flavor of ice cream, you get to choose between two or more flavors that you like. You can try to organize your different options into what will work, what you don't think will work, and what might be able to work. Once this is laid out, this will help you to look at everything objectively before making decisions.

## Make Your Decisions Informed

Before you make any kind of decision you can ask questions of someone who has to make the decision with you, or you can just spend time asking questions in general. Your job is to take in as much information as possible before you decide on anything.

For example, a good thing to consider is who is going to benefit the most if you make one decision over another? If you were leaning towards one decision over another, why is that? Will one decision end up with more work to complete compared to others? The point of asking these questions is to think things through before you make any sort of choice at all.

## Consider a Second Opinion

Making certain decisions can be hard. The good news is that you don't have to always make the decisions on your own. You can always benefit from getting a second opinion. If you look for a second opinion, make sure that this opinion is from someone you trust. This person can be your friend, a family member, or even an expert you can call if you have these connections.

The point here is to get the opinion from someone who may be separate to the actual problem. They may be able to look at it from a different point of view and can discuss the various options with you. Even if you don't pick the decision that you get from them, asking someone else to help you with decisions can help you pick the best choice overall.

## Decide with Logic and Leave the Emotion Behind

There will be some instances where we will get caught up in the moment letting our emotions get the better of us. When this happens, we usually start to make rash and ill-advised decisions due to pride, sadness, and even anger. When it comes to making good decisions, your emotions can have a very dangerous influence on you.

This is because you are going to just jump on the first decision that pops into your head, without thinking it through.

Before you decide to make any decisions, it is important to take a break and ensure that your emotions are not causing any issues and messing with your logic. Before you decide, take a deep breath and work on clearing your mind so that the emotions never get in the way of your judgment. Once you are sure those emotions are gone or have subsided, your logic should be clear and you're ready to move forward from this point.

## Learn from Your Bad Decisions

No matter how hard you work on your critical thinking, there will always be times when you make decisions that are often not the right ones. This is just a part of life. But that shouldn't stop us from thinking carefully on the next problem we face. There are so many decisions that we have to make in our daily lives, and it is impossible for us to pick the right choice each time. What we need to do here is to be ready to accept failure when it happens. Yes, accepting failure can be hard to handle. No one likes it. But when you learn how to accept it and take it gracefully, you can learn a lot that will help you to make the right choices in the future.

## How to Make Better Decisions

All of us want to the ability and confidence to make better decisions in our lives. Learning how to improve our decision-making skills so that we can make the best choices is something that we'd all love to do. Here are some of the ways that you can ensure to make better decisions in your day to day life:

1. **Make all the decisions in the morning.** Morning is often the best time to make some of your biggest decisions. This is due to the benefit of having a combination of dopamine and serotonin which helps avoid the issue of decision fatigue. If you do need to make a

bigger decision later on in the day, then taking a nap or at least taking a break can help to reset the brain.

2. **Eat first.** Making decisions when you are hungry can be almost impossible. It affects the way you think. Try to get all of your physical desires taken care of before you start on your daily work or tasks.

3. **Cut down how many choices you get.** Sometimes, we get overwhelmed when we have too many choices to decide on. Limiting ourselves to just a few choices as soon as possible can ensure that making a decision is much easier.

4. **Open up the windows.** Adding some extra oxygen to the home can help you to make better decisions, and also adding plants around the house can help aswell.

# Decision-Making in the Workplace and Life

While there are a lot of important decisions that you will need to make in your own personal life, there are also a lot of times when you must make critical decisions in your workplace. This can be difficult a lot of the time due to the people your work with. Whether it is a big business or a small one, there are always others who will need to agree to the decisions so everyone can work together on the decision being implemented.

It is important that the information is shared between everyone, and that everyone gets a chance to vote and give their opinion before any decision is agreed upon. Some of the steps that you can take in order to ensure strong and sound decisions are made in the workplace include:

1. **Decide how important the decision is.** Our modern world is always busy and many things feel rushed. We get into the mindset that each decision has to be done right now, as soon as

possible. But in reality, some decisions need more time than others. Take a step back from the problem and then decide how urgent and important the decision really is.

2. **Consider a large range of options for decision-making.** Depending on the project, you may want to work with a consensus, a vote, or a subgroup or a single person to decide. All of them can be effective, but you will have to decide what is the best option for you and the situation you're in.

3. **Make sure that you define things up front.** This should be done especially if you are working with a consensus. For example, you may decide that you are going to continue on with a debate and the exploration until everyone is fully supportive of the final decision. In some cases, they can drag on for some time. Or, if you find that you have a limited time for the decision-making, you may want to put a deadline on reaching a consensus.

4. **Make sure the right people are in the process.** You should include those who are

going to make the decision, along with those who are going to implement the solution and anyone else who will be affected by the solution and the decision.

5. **Make all of the data that you have available**. You may find that you don't have all the data, but make sure that all of the data that you have is out in the open to help you make an informed a decision. If you feel that you are stuck, then you need to look for more research. If possible, also look at the data that includes the sense of security, wishes, and fears of those in the business. All of these can play into the decision that you go with.

6. **Estimate a deadline for the decision.** You should also consider letting others know the deadline ahead of time. If you find that the decision needs to be delayed, then make sure that you update others. And once you find that the decision is made, ensure that everyone knows what it is.

7. **Expect that there will be some struggle**. No matter what the situation is and the decision

you make, expect that there will be some sort of struggle involved. It isn't easy to get through this, but it is a valuable part of the process and one that you shouldn't just skip over.

## Techniques to Improve Your Decision-making Abilities

Decision-making is an important part of our lives. We are constantly surrounded by decisions that we need to follow all of the time. Whether we are deciding on a big move for a new job, whether to start a family or not, what clothes to wear, or what to enjoy for supper, there are always a million things that we need to decide on from one day to the next.

Decision-making can be hard, even though we spend a lot of time concentrating and focusing on it each day. Being able to improve our decision-making abilities can often help us learn the best way to make smart decisions for our needs and can make it so much easier to pick what is right for us, whilst saving a ton of time. Some of the techniques that you can use to help improve your decision-making abilities include:

## Stop Delaying

Over time, you will find that the simple decisions are the most fun. You can just simply write them on your to-do list and tick them off as you go. When you feel that the stakes increase and you are now faced with making some critical decisions, keep up the same process of getting through things quickly. Never delay just because a decision seems more difficult.

If you struggle with this, then schedule some time to work on the risks, outcomes, and pros and cons that come with your decision. Consider the second and third order effects of your decision, if you can, during this session. Remember that it is always better to make a decision right away. Nothing ever gets done when you sweep the problem under the rug.

## Put the Emotions and Ego Away

Decision-making is sometimes difficult because you often let yourself become too invested personally on how this decision is going to make you feel and look. You can still solve the problem in an objective way, but you have to learn how to listen to your logic instead of emotions and ego. One method of doing this is to list out the potential causes and put your emotion and ego on the back burner.

You will be able to make better decisions when you can focus your energy on the facts, rather than looking at any personal deficiencies that may be there.

## Always Question the Data You Have

To make informed decisions, you need to ensure that you do a lot of research. You need to find the right information so that you can look through it and get all the points of view before you get started. Another step that you need to take here is to question the data that you receive.

With the rise of the Internet, there is lots of data that you can look up. But that doesn't mean that the information you find is going to be legitimate. Before you decide to use some information to make a decision, you must make sure that you question the data that you have. Check and see if there are any other documents that can support the information that you are working with. Check to see if it matches up with the information that you have already found and if it is unbiased and actually has a good argument associated with it. This helps you to learn whether the information is critical and useful for the decision you are trying to make.

## Understand the Risks

The final step and technique to work on here are to plan for all of the risks that can happen with any kind of decision that you decide to make. One way to think about this is to plan for doomsday. Take about ten minutes to look at your problem and then consider the worst-case scenario about any decision that you want to make.

For example, let's say that you need to fire someone from your business. With this technique, you would consider what would be the worst thing that could happen from doing this? There are a lot of ways that you can mitigate the risk of each kind of decision, but you need to take some time to figure out these risks so that you can mitigate the risks and avoid them as much as possible. Try to know the risks from the beginning making the situation easiest to handle as possible.

# Chapter 7
# Problem-Solving

The next thing that we need to explore is the idea of problem-solving. Problem solving is something that a lot of people struggle with and lack. Some find that their decision-making skills are not always as good as they think they are, and really don't know what to do about it.

The ability to use problem-solving to help you deal with anything that comes your way can be a critical skill that you can utilize on a daily basis. The good news is that anyone can actually learn to improve their problem-solving skills, no matter how bad they currently are. Let's take a look at some of the basics that you should know about problem-solving and how you can go about improving them.

# What Is Problem-Solving?

Before we get too far into this chapter, it is important to understand more about this topic. Problem-solving is one of the methods we are going to use to understand what is happening to us in our environment, in identifying the things that we wish to change around us, and to figure out the steps we need to take to get the outcome we desire. Problem-solving is so important; it is the source of all the new inventions that we see around us---the social and cultural evolution---and it can be the basis for market-based economies. When it is used properly, it can be effective at helping with continuous learning, communication, and improvement.

Since problem-solving is so important to many aspects of our daily lives, it is crucial that we learn more about it. Problem-solving is the process of taking observations of what goes on in the environment around us, identifying what you can improve or even change, performing diagnostics on why things are in their current state, developing the alternatives and approaches needed in order to create change, making decisions about which alternative to select out of several, and then taking action to ensure those changes get implemented. And to finish it off, the problem solver will often take the time to observe the impact of those actions to see if they are really successful.

Each step used in problem-solving employs a variety of methods and skills that will help you be more effective to the change that you want, and it can even help you to determine the level of problem complexity that you can address.

Many of us have learned how to solve problems from an early age. We have learnt how to eat, to talk, how to coordinate the movements we do when walking, and even how to communicate. As we progress through our lives, you will work more and more on your problem-solving skills, making them become more refined, matured, and even more sophisticated. This results in us being able to solve problems that are increasingly more difficult.

Problem-solving can be a challenging process, but individuals, as well as companies, will be able to use it in order to exert more control over their environment.

Both business and personal environments are going to be full of processes, interactions, activities, and broken things or at least don't operate in the way that they should. Using the skills that come with problem-solving can give us the tools that we need in order to identify these things, figure out why they don't work properly, and then how we can determine the right action and steps we should take to fix them.

Then, we need to move on to addressing the risks. Humans are adept at learning to find trends, and they can become more aware of any cause and effect relationships that show up in the world around them. These skills can be important because they are used to help us to fix anything that breaks, but they also allow us to make predictions on what is going to happen later on. We are able to do this based on current events and past experiences. The skills that come with problem-solving can be applied to help us anticipate future events and can ensure that we can take action in the present to change future results.

For example, if we know that a machine will often break down at the end of the year, unless we change one of the filters or one of the parts, we may make plans to get that part fixed ahead of time. This helps the machine to keep on working without causing a delay in production or causing a lot of people standing around and not getting things done during work time.

Another thing that problem-solving can help with is to improve performance. Companies and individuals are not going to exist in complete isolation from the rest of the world. There is a complex web of relationships, one that is always changing. As a result of this, the actions that one person uses will often have a direct impact on others in the group, or it could indirectly impact things by changing the dynamics of the environment.

These connections are going to be there no matter what you try to do. And these types of interdependencies enable humans to work together so that they can solve and figure out the more complex problems, while also creating a force that ensures everyone improves their performance and forces them to adapt the improvements that others do. Problem-solving can help us understand the relationships and implement the changes and improvements that are needed to stay competitive and to survive in an environment that is always changing.

And finally, the other thing that problem-solving can help out with is seizing the opportunities. Problem-solving isn't always about responding and fixing the environment that is around us at this moment. It can also be about innovating what there is, creating something that is new and even changing up the environment to make sure it is desirable. Using problem-solving can help us to identify and exploit opportunities that occur in the environment so that we can make predictions and keep control over what is going to happen to us in the future.

As you can see, problem-solving, both its processes and skills, are going to be a very important part of your daily life, whether you are a company or an individual. Developing and then refining these skills through training, learning, and practice can ensure that you are able to solve any problem that you encounter effectively. And with time and practice, you will be able to take on problems that are higher in difficulty and complexity.

## Why People Struggle with Problem-Solving

Many people find that they aren't good at problem-solving. Many times, facing problems is going to bring out emotions that we would rather avoid. But being able to solve a problem effectively can be an important skill to help you create the perfect life that you want to have. Avoiding problems simply because you don't like the process of problem-solving just means that any issue you are dealing with could get worse.

You will find that, many times, those who are more emotionally sensitive are the ones who are the most creative when it comes to problem-solving. This is usually because they want to avoid the issues that come with those emotions, so they will often look for solutions that others may not even consider or think about.

But there are also people who seem to have trouble with problem-solving no matter what. This may be due to their natural problem-solving ability being damaged by various life situations, which may have caused them to develop a type of fear any time that they run into some kind of problem they need to solve.

Going back to those who are more emotionally sensitive, problem-solving can be stifled when they receive feedback. For these particular types of individuals, when it comes to receiving feedback from those whom they love, it will often hit them hard emotionally. If you have had issues with people in the past criticizing your problem-solving skills or criticizing the ideas you might have had for others, you may have been made to feel disheartened and put off offering suggestions or ever putting any of your problem-solving ideas into action.

So, even though these emotionally sensitive people are more likely to come up with creative solutions to their problems, more than often they will come unstuck when it comes to problem-solving because they worry too much about what other people may think of them and their ideas. If they can learn to care less about what others think and not let them be influenced by this, their problem-solving skills would become a lot more effective as a result.

You may also find that your own emotions, whether you are emotionally sensitive or not, can be an issue with your problem-solving skills. If your always saying things like "I don't know what to do" because you have the fear that your sibling is going to be upset with you, then the biggest issue you are dealing with here is that you don't want to handle the emotions that come with the best solution.

Emotions are not always a bad thing. These emotions can sometimes give you helpful information that you can consider, but for most of the time we become victims of our emotions which lead us into not living a life we really want. Picking a choice because you are scared of how the other person will react, avoiding something because it makes you sad, or having an unjustified fear that you won't be able to pass a test can be examples of your emotions getting in the way of you choosing the best solution. No matter what problems you are dealing with, you always need to consider what emotions are at play and make sure that they don't get in the way of the best solution.

Over time, you may consider that you cannot always manage the emotions that you have when you feel unsure about the way you react to any kind of situation, or that you cannot predict the way that certain emotions may affect the behavior that you exhibit. If so, you are more likely to avoid any new ideas and situations. This drives us to stick with the familiar, not because it is the best, but because it is the familiar and what we are used to.

You may also have had a problem where you have received feedback accusing you of being wrong in the way that you feel or think. This can happen often to those who are emotionally sensitive. For these people, especially if the feedback they receive tells them they are always wrong, it is easy to look to others to help determine how realistic or valuable your ideas are. In some cases, you may even start to depend on others to help you figure out all your problems because your now led to believe that you can't do this on your own. Basically, what you have learnt in all of this is to just be passive.

If you have tried to work on problem-solving in the past, but all its does is cause you bigger problems, or you find that others chastise you for your efforts, you start to believe that you cannot solve a problem on your own because you will always be wrong. You will start to spend your time seeing who will solve your problems for you. Your usual reactions to a problem may be something like "Tell me what to do, just tell me what to do" or "I don't know what to do".

If any of these descriptions tend to describe you, then there is still things you can do to help. Problem-solving is a skill and a process that you can learn. The first step that you must work on is figuring out how to regulate your emotions so that you can think clearly and use coping skills that are the most effective for your needs. Everyone can learn how to work on their problem-solving skills, they may just need to learn how to avoid the emotions more or at least limit them as much as possible, and learn that they can actually handle their own problems without having to rely on anyone else.

# The Process of Problem-Solving

The process of problem-solving is a mental process that involves discovering, analyzing, and then solving a variety of problems. You will usually just work on one problem at a time, but sometimes, there may be a few problems that relate to each other that you can work on together at the same time. The end goal with problem-solving is to overcome any obstacles that you are facing so you can find a solution that will help resolve the issue.

Choosing the best strategy that you should use for solving any problem is often going to depend on the situation. In some situations, people see that learning everything they can about an issue or problem using this knowledge to come up with a solution is the best option. In other cases, it is better to try and get an insight or use creativity to come up with the best solution.

Now, there are a few steps that you can take when it comes down to problem-solving. Regardless of the different problems that you may be faced with, the process for problem-solving is the same each time. To solve any problem that you encounter correctly, it is important that you follow a series of steps. These steps are often known as the problem-solving cycle, which will include coming up with the right strategies for a solution and how to organize your knowledge.

While this is a cycle portrayed sequentially, there can be a lot of variations and movements in the way people go about following these steps. Instead, we will more than often skip these steps or go through the same steps a few times until the right solution is reached. Some of the steps that are shown in the problem-solving cycle include:

The first step is to identify the problem. While this is a step that may seem pretty obvious, you may find that identifying the problem is sometimes more complicated than it seems. In some cases, you may make the mistake when identifying the wrong source of the problem, doing this will just make any attempts you use to solve the problem useless and inefficient. Finding the right problem and the source of that problem can help put you on the right path.

The next step that you should work on is defining your problem. Once you can identify your problem or the issue that you should work on, it is time to define the problem. If you have a full definition of the problem that you are working on, then you will be able to solve it a lot quicker.

Now, we need to work on forming our strategy. It is important for you to come up with a good and effective strategy that will help you to solve the problem. The approach that you will use can depend on your own personal preferences as well as the situation that you are trying to work on. During this time, you will also need to organize the information you will use for your strategy. Before you can come up with a good solution, you first need to organize all of the available information. Think about what you know concerning the problem and even the things that you don't know.

The more information that you can gather, the easier it is to prepare and come up with a good solution.

Another thing that you can work on is allocating the resources that you have. No one has an unlimited amount of time, money, and resources in order to solve any problem, no matter how important that problem is. before you even get started with solving this problem, you must determine how important and urgent this problem is. If you find that it is really important, you will want to allocate extra resources. If it is something that you need to work on but is not a high priority, then you can allocate your resources a bit differently.

At this point, you should have a good solution in place. Whether you figured out the right solution on your own or with the help of others, you should have explored a few different possibilities in order to help. Now, it is time to monitor your progress. Those who are effective at problem-solving will make sure that they monitor their progress while they work towards their solution. If you find that you aren't making any progress towards your goal, then you might need to relook at the whole strategy and see if you need to change your approach.

And finally, it is always useful to evaluate the results you get. After you pick out your solution and have implemented, it is important to take some time to evaluate the results. This helps you to figure out if the solution you chose was the right one for this problem. Sometimes, the evaluation is right away, and other times you may wait until the solution has some time to work before doing the evaluation.

## Problem-Solving in the Workplace and in Life

In addition to working with problem-solving in your own personal life, there may be times when you need to work on your problem-solving skills in your workplace. Sometimes, this can just be things like finishing up a project efficiently and on time, and in other cases these skills need to be used in order to help avoid a crisis. Being able to recognize the various examples of problem-solving in the workplace can help you prepare more for work-related issues. Let's look at a few examples of how this can work as well as some of the techniques that you can use for you to do well with problem-solving in the workplace.

## Brainstorming

You will find that there are many instances where the workplace can benefit from new ideas of the team. And to come up with these new ideas, you will need to work on brainstorming. Everyone on the team, from the staff to the management, would need to come into the room. They can have a piece of paper to start. Then, given a time limit, they should start to write down any idea that comes into their mind. There are no bad answers here, just have them write down whatever they think about because no one else will see the paper if they don't want to share it.

After everyone has a chance to write down their ideas, the group will share these ideas and then expand on what they see as the best ideas until they come up with the basis of their solution. Make sure that everyone on the team and everyone in the room has a chance to share their ideas to help with the creativity. Brainstorming can be a great way for you to get input from many different people, providing you with more solutions to help you succeed.

## Delegation

Each person in the group will need to work with their own set of responsibilities. The responsibilities that they get will be based on the educational background and experience that each person has. There should never be the issue with one person taking on all of the work that comes with a project. Once a solution is figured out, you can take some time to discuss the different tasks to complete that solution, and then determine who will be in charge of each part. Make sure that the meeting doesn't end without everyone knowing what job and task they need to work on.

## Committees

You may find that working with a committee can work either in a permanent or, sometimes, temporary position. The committee can be a workgroup responsible for handling specific issues in the workplace. For example, if your department for logistics runs into some challenges with one of your shipping companies, then it may be possible to create a committee that helps you to look into what this issue is and what is causing it before coming up with the proper solution.

It is pretty common for these committees to include employees with specific skills which are needed to get the job done. The committee that you use to deal with the shipping issue above will probably include a representative that works with the problem company, one that works with a better shipping company, and the shipping manager since these individuals know how to handle these kinds of situations.

## Evaluations

During problem-solving, evaluations on a regular basis are always important. Taking the time to monitor department progress and employee progress versus the goals of the company is a constant problem-solving process in the workplace, and it is very important when you want to maintain productivity. These evaluations can be used by managers to help compare actual performance against any of the goals that are found in the business plan of a company or maybe in their marketing plan.

The analysis of these results can be used in order to get a good idea of the issues that should be addressed, and then the team or the management can use this to create the perfect plan to address the issues. Let's say that the revenue of a business is falling and it is lower than the projections of the company for the year. There would then be an evaluation done on the company's sales process to reveal any shortcomings that may show up in the sales methods that should be corrected in order to get the revenue on track to where it should be.

## Useful Problem-Solving Skills and How to Develop Them

When it comes to problem-solving, there are actually a few key skills that you need to work on in order to make it easier to solve any problem you encounter. Some of the skills that you need when learning to develop better problem-solving skills include:

1. **Creativity:** Most of the time a problem is going to be solved either systematically or intuitively. Intuition can be used when you don't need to find any new knowledge. You already have the information that you need to make a quick decision and solve the problem, or you can at least use your experience or your common sense to do so. Sometimes, problems that are more

complex or that you have never worked on before will need a more systematic approach, and this will often need some creative thinking to help you out.

2. **Researching Skills:** Being able to define and solve any problem that you have can often require you to research. Sometimes, the research is simple, and you can just get away with a quick search on Google. But there are also times when the research project will be more in-depth and rigorous to find the answers that you need.

3. **Teamworking:** You will find that many problems are going to be defined and solved the best when you get input from others. Teamworking may just sound like something that you do at work, but you will find that it can be important at school and at home as well. If you cannot work in a team, then it may be time to work on this in order to help with your critical thinking.

4. **Emotional Intelligence:** Emotional intelligence is very important when it comes to becoming a critical thinker. The emotional intelligence that you have, as well as the ability to recognize the emotions of others, will help you to guide you to an appropriate solution. If you can solve a problem in the right manner, without worrying about emotions getting in the way, then you will find things can be much easier to decide.

5. **Risk Management:** Solving a variety of problems will always involve a certain amount of risk. You always need to weigh the risk against the idea of not solving a problem ahead of time.

6. **Decision-Making:** Decision-making and problem-solving are often closely related. And being able to make a decision can be very important when it comes to finding various options and alternatives. You need to be able to

research and figure out the best solution based on the information that you are given.

# Techniques to Develop Your Problem-Solving Abilities

Now that we have taken some time to discuss problem-solving and some of the skills that are needed to help with this, it is time to work on the best techniques needed to develop these abilities. There are many different techniques that can help, but we are going to look at the top six effective ways to enhance your problem-solving skills to help you get started.

## Focus Less on the Problem and More on the Solution

Studies have been proven that the brain cannot find solutions if you focus all of your energy on a problem. The reason for this is that when you focus just on a problem, you are just feeding the brain negativity. This will just cause you to build up negative emotions which will hinder your thinking ability.

This doesn't mean that you get to ignore the problem you are dealing with. But don't let it bother you to the extent where you're getting stressed out. Instead, try to think about it calmly so you don't start the spiral that we have just mentioned. It can help out in many cases to acknowledge the problem first, and then, while remaining calm, move the focus to more of a solution-oriented mindset where you keep fixed on the possible solution, rather than focusing on what went wrong or who might be at fault.

## Adapt the Five Why's

The five why's can be very helpful no matter what kind of problem you are dealing with, you may have heard about them being used before in business and other situations. This requires you to ask why about a problem at least five times. The more that you can ask this question, the closer you will get to the proper solution. You don't have to limit yourself to five times, but it is known as the five why's to encourage you to ask why at least this amount of times.

When you repeatedly ask yourself the question of why on one problem, then you can dig deeper into the root cause of a problem. You may find a ton of solutions for a problem, but if you don't discover the root of that problem, then it's likely that you are not finding the proper solution for your needs.

Let's look at an example of how this can work. Let's say, our problem is that we always show up late for work. The way that you can implement the five why's with this includes:

1. Why am I late to work? I always hear the alarm and click on the snooze button so that I can go back to sleep.

2. Why do I want to keep on sleeping in the morning? I still feel tired when it is time to wake up.

3. Why do I feel tired in the morning? I stayed up too late the night before so I am now tired.

4. Why did I go to bed late the night before? I didn't feel too sleepy at bedtime, but that was

probably because I was drinking coffee. I also spent a lot of time scrolling on Facebook or another social media site and couldn't stop.

5.  Why did I decide to drink the coffee? Because I felt really sleepy the day before and had trouble staying awake at work, so I drank the coffee.

With this option, you can see that you have the solution and have put yourself into a vicious cycle here. If you didn't go that far to find the root of the problem, you may have decided to just set a few more alarms and then been up every five minutes in the morning. You can instead stop surfing endlessly on Facebook at night so that you can get to bed, feel more energetic during the day, and don't need to rely on the coffee that keeps you awake.

## Simplify as Much as Possible

Even though simplicity is the best, we often have a tendency to over complicate things. If you are working on a problem and can't seem to come up with the right solution, then it maybe time to try to simplify your approach.

Take a look at the problem and try to remove as many details as possible, bringing yourself back to the basics. Try looking for a really easy and obvious solution. And this can lead you to be surprised by the results. You already know that the simple things are the most productive, and this can be true with your problem as well.

## List out as Many of the Solutions as you Can

When you are problem-solving, make sure that you entertain all of the solutions that you can find. Even if you think that the solution seems a little silly at first, you need to keep an open mind about everything. Even if you don't end up using a particular solution, you may find that it is the springboard you need to trigger the solution you pick.

During this stage, make sure that you keep your mind open and never ridicule yourself when the solution may seem stupid. The crazy and silly ideas are the ones that often trigger the more viable and better solutions that you end up choosing.

## Think Laterally

Sometimes, the best way to come up with the solution to your problem is to think laterally. For this one, consider the saying "You can't dig a hole in a different place by digging it deeper." What this means is that you should work to change your approach and see if you can look at it in a new way.

You can flip the objective around and see if there is some kind of solution to the problem, even if that solution is the polar opposite of where you were looking.

## Use Language That Opens up New Doors

Another solution that you can work with is using the right kind of language. Often, our language, whether we speak it out loud or in our heads, is negative and can make it harder to come up with the solution that we need. You should always lead your thinking with some phrases like "what if" and "imagine if". These terms can open up the brains ability to think more so that we can think in a more creative way which will encourage better solutions. Make sure you avoid negative and closed language like "This is not right, but" or "I don't think" because this will only limit your way of thinking.

Problem-solving can be difficult. You will always want to try and come up with the best solution for the situation that you are in, but you may be limited to the options that you can be or the solutions you can find. Using the tips and techniques in this chapter can help you find the perfect solution, no matter what.

# Conclusion

Thanks for making it through to the end of the book. We hope it was informative and able to provide you with all of the tools you need to achieve your goals whatever they may be.

The next step is to begin using the critical thinking skills that we have discussed in this guide to help you make more informed decisions throughout your life. While critical thinking doesn't have to be used all the time, you will find that there are many scenarios and situations in our lives when we could definitely think more critically to get better results.

This guide has spent some time looking at the basics of critical thinking and how it can be used to improve your own life. By the time you are done, you will have a better understanding of what this skill is about and why it is so important for you to use. You will also know the best times to utilize critical thinking to get the best results in your life as possible.

Finally, if you found this book useful in any way, a review on Amazon is always appreciated!

Printed in Great Britain
by Amazon